102 ART JOKES FOR YOU

A DEFINITIVE GUIDE TO CRACKING A SMILE WITH ARTISTIC STYLE

ELAINE HAMMERMASTER GODINEZ

ISBN: 978-0-9773205-1-6

To artists and art students everywhere:
Make laughter and art everyday.
That seems like a pretty great life.

———

For Trevor and Vincent

Beautiful lives are not always long—but they touch others—
and other lives become more beautiful because of them.

**What did Matisse's doctor say when
Matisse was too old to paint?**

Cut it out!

FUN FACT

Henri Matisse (French artist, 1869-1954) used color brilliantly in his paintings and artwork. He turned to cutting out paper shapes and making beautiful **collages** when he was older and his hands were too stiff to paint.

2

What did the circle say to the triangle?

Meet me at the corner!

102 ART JOKES FOR YOU

FUN FACT

Circles and triangles are **geometric shapes**.

3

Why did the artist use neon colors in his painting?

Because he had a bright idea

FUN FACT

The color of **neon** gas is actually bright red. Artists can make neon light sculptures, but most of us think of neon as extremely bright pigment paint colors and drawing materials.

4

Why did the artist use a paintbrush to draw in an elevator?

He wanted to brush up on his drawing skills

FUN FACT

The first known **paintbrush** was probably invented in China about 300 BC.

5

Why did the circle stay home?

He didn't want to be a "round" people

FUN FACT

Walt Disney (American artist, 1901-1966) said that his animated cartoon character, Mickey Mouse, was based off of a friendly shape—the **circle**.

**What was Edvard Munch's
favorite dessert?**

I scream

FUN FACT

Edvard Munch (Norwegian artist, 1863-1944) best known work is entitled, *The Scream.* It is one of the most well-known paintings in the world today.

What question did red ask yellow when they met up?

Orange you happy we got together?

FUN FACT

Red and yellow are **primary** colors on the color wheel. When they are mixed, they create the **secondary** color—orange.

8

**What was Leonardo da Vinci's favorite
meal of the day?**

The Last Supper

FUN FACT

Leonardo da Vinci (Italian artist, 1452-1519) spent two years painting a **mural,** which is a big painting on a wall, called *The Last Supper*. It is one of the world's most recognized paintings. Leonardo was also **ambidextrous**. That means he was able to draw and write with either of his hands. Try it. Make a drawing with your other hand!

What did the pyramid say to the cube?

You are missing the point!

FUN FACT

A **pyramid** and a **cube** are geometric forms. **Forms** are important in learning how to draw, so that things appear three dimensional or **3D**. Did you know that a cube is actually made up of three identical pyramids?

10

Why did Monet get up first thing in the morning to paint the sunrise?

He wanted to make a good first impression!

FUN FACT

Claude Monet (French artist, 1840-1926) his painting, *Impression, Sunrise,* was important. It was the reason why a whole group of artists were called **Impressionists**. Impressionist artists painted with a style of mostly choppy or blurry brushstrokes and captured the effects of light into their paintings.

11

What object is king in an art class?

The ruler

FUN FACT

Rulers are useful tools for artists to draw straight lines and measure. People like to say, "I can't even draw a straight line!" But of course they can—if they have a ruler! Artists enjoy drawing **freehand**—without rulers, tracing or other guides. It's okay if everything is not perfect or straight. Just draw and enjoy!

12

Why did the bronze statue show up at the movie set?

It thought it was a part of the cast!

FUN FACT

Statues made out of **bronze**, a metal made up of 10% tin and 90% copper, have been around since the early Greeks made them in about 475 BC. They poured the hot metal into a **cast** or a mold—kind of like pouring cake batter into a cake pan—and that is basically how they made bronze statues.

13

What do the rainbow police do to art criminals?

They send them to prism!

FUN FACT

A **prism,** in the form of a transparent glass triangular prism, will take sunlight and disperse the light passing through it into the **spectrum** of full **rainbow** colors. Then you can see all the wavelengths of light colors present in white light broken out. It's pretty spectacular. Try it.

14

Why was Jackson Pollack's style of painting so different?

Because it was in a whole different splatter-gory!

FUN FACT

Jackson Pollack (American artist, 1912-1956) is most known for his technique of painting by splattering or pouring paint onto big canvases on the floor. They called this style **Abstract Expressionism**. He wasn't painting a kitty or a tree—or anything recognizable. He was just exploring colors and organic shapes made by the paint splatters. Pretty fun. Try it.

15

What do you call it when school paint gets angry?

A tempera tantrum!

FUN FACT

Everyone remembers the unique smell of school tempera paint! Did you know that the first tempera paint was originally made with eggs? Called **Egg Tempera**. Just don't eat it for breakfast. Tempera paint is not edible!

16

What did purple say to yellow?

"I can never say 'No' to a complement!"

FUN FACT

Colors directly across the color wheel from each other—like purple (also known as violet) and yellow—are called **complementary colors**. They are opposites. But they bring out the best in each other. When next to each other, they will make the other color it's strongest—with good contrast. Kind of like people's personalities sometimes!

17

What do you call it when a pencil is mad at lined grid paper?

A graph-fight!

FUN FACT

Graph paper is useful for many art tasks. Artists enjoy the use of a **grid** in designing, structuring or enlarging drawings. The grid lines and squares help the artist with proportion. Did you know grids have even been found in cave paintings? **Graphite** is the blackish substance used in pencils to make drawing marks.

18

Why were Picasso's portraits of gossips?

Because they were two faced

FUN FACT

Pablo Picasso (Spanish artist, 1881-1973) was known for creating the style of art called **Cubism**. His Cubist **portraits** showed the person from different angles all in one image. Sometimes it appeared as if they had two different faces in the same painting!

19

How can you tell when your Crayolas are tired?

You see a cra-yawn!

FUN FACT

Most of us love crayons. Cheerful and colorful, they are one of our first drawing tools. Maybe they are a form of aromatherapy for artists. That means the smell of crayons makes you feel happy!

20

What do you call a painting of soda?

Pop Art

FUN FACT

People in America call carbonated sweet drinks Soda or Pop. However, **Pop Art** is the name of a style of art that was new in the 1950's. Artists like **Andy Warhol** (American artist, 1928-1981) took simple, bright images of popular things in life around them, and made art images from them. What is something popular today you can make a fun image of? Try it!

21

**What do you call a bearded
ceramics teacher?**

Harry Potter

FUN FACT

The word, **Ceramics,** comes from the Greek word that means pottery. **Pottery** can be made out of different things—but we mostly think of **clay**. Ceramic art pieces can be useful like a cup to drink out of—but also can just be decorative and beautiful to the eye. You might call someone who makes ceramics a "potter."

22

**Why did green, violet and orange think
someone was plotting against them?**

They overheard someone mention
a color scheme!

FUN FACT

A scheme sometimes means a devious plan. However, **color schemes** are not devious! They are very useful arrangements of colors for artists. For instance, green, violet and orange create a color scheme called **Triadic**— that means they form an equidistant triangle relationship on the color wheel. Artists use these color relationships—or color schemes—for creating different effects in their art.

23

**What did they call angry Marcel
Duchamp going downstairs?**

Rude Descending a Staircase

FUN FACT

Marcel Duchamp (French-American artist, 1887-1968) most famous painting is called *Nude Descending a Staircase, No. 2.* It is an abstracted depiction of a person walking downstairs, so actually, you can't see anything in detail. There is nudity in art through history. It may be part of the study and presentation of the human form, or an artist may have other reasons to use it. When you visit an Art Museum don't be surprised to see all kinds of art. Anyway, some people at first didn't like this painting, it made them uncomfortable. It is famous today. Along with his re-make of the Mona Lisa with a mustache and a goatee. Why do you think he painted and created these interesting images? How would you re-do the Mona Lisa? Maybe give her a new hairdo! Try it.

24

Where did two artists meet and create a magic trick?

At the vanishing point!

FUN FACT

A **vanishing point** is important in many works of art. Basically, it is the point on the horizon where things in a drawing disappear or vanish. In a **one point perspective** drawing, all the **parallel** sight lines converge together at this point. Things get smaller and smaller along the sight lines leading into the vanishing point. Try a simple one-point perspective drawing of a road vanishing into the distance.

25

What did the artist say when he finished his carving?

What a relief!

FUN FACT

The word **relief** is from a Latin word that means "to raise." This is a **sculpture technique** where sculpted areas remain attached to their solid base, so it appears as if the sculpted part is rising up out of the base. Carving usually involves using some sort of sharp tool. Kids: Don't try carving alone. But you can create a relief—raised up area—in a piece of art with dried glue or other materials. Always ask for help from your art teacher or parent with art tools and techniques that involve sharp tools or materials that aren't labeled non-toxic. Be safe!

26

Why did the artist flunk his art exam?

He drew a blank.

FUN FACT

I never give my students art exams—so no one ever draws a blank!

27

**What did they say when Seurat's
painting was erased?**

It's utterly pointless!

FUN FACT

Georges Seurat (French painter, 1859-1891) was known for creating a style of painting called **Pointillism**. His most famous painting is called, *A Sunday Afternoon on the Island of La Grande Jatte.* In this painting, you can see thousands of tiny dots of paint marks right next to each other. These dots make up the entire image of people enjoying activities on a beautiful, pleasant Sunday by the waterside. Try it. Make a painting with tiny dots of colors.

28

**What did the drawing pinned to the
bulletin board say?**

Oh no! I'm under a tack!

FUN FACT

Make sure you display some of your art. Your art is an expression of **you**. It has no need to be judged. It is simply to be valued as being art—**a visual personal expression**. It validates your creativity and effort. Other people can see it too and appreciate your efforts. Or not. Not everyone may like your art. That's okay. If it matters a lot what other people think—perhaps you should rethink that. Many artists were attacked by critics. That means some people said they didn't like their art. The artists continued to create anyway! Create your art your own way. That is what great artists do.

29

What kind of an artist is a cat with paint on it's paws?

A printmaker

FUN FACT

A lot of people don't know much about **printmaking**. It has a huge part in art history. A print is usually when you make an image and it is transferred to a piece of paper or other surface by ink. My favorite printmaker of all time is **Johannes Gutenburg** (German printer, c.1400-1468) because his invention of movable type and the basic printing press changed the world drastically. For the first time, books could be produced with illustrations for everyone to have. Up until then, books were written and illustrated by hand and very few people had them. Can you imagine how much artwork and books have been printed since then? Thanks, Johannes! That's huge!

What did the bank thief say to his partner?

Let's grab the Monet and Gogh!

FUN FACT

So many Monet and van Gogh jokes! I have a few more up my art sleeve.

31

Is turquoise the best color?

Yes. It is cyan-tifically proven.

FUN FACT

Cyan is a bright blue-green color. It is important for being one of the three colors used in light and printing primaries: yellow, magenta and cyan. I can't say turquoise is the best color—think of all the other colors that would be jealous!

32

**Why didn't the weaving want to be hung
on the wall?**

Because it didn't want to loom
over anyone

FUN FACT

Weaving is a great art technique. Weaving has been used for practical items like baskets and clothing. Sometimes weavings are just beautiful to look at like wall hangings or tapestries. One of the tools sometimes used in weaving is called a **loom**. It has notches to hold thread or yarn—the **warp** threads—so that the **weft** threads can easily be woven through.

33

**How is a drawing artist's
quesadilla served?**

On a tortillon!

FUN FACT

A **tortillon** is a hollow drawing tool made up of rolled paper and tapered at one end. It is similar to a **blending stump** which also, like a tortillon, is used to blend and smudge pencil or charcoal marks in a drawing. Have you ever used one? Try it.

34

What do you call a fancy artistic cup of hot chocolate?

Rococo with marshmallows

FUN FACT

Rococo is a style of art and decoration with fancy scrolling curves and elaborate ornaments made popular around 1730. Think of big golden gilded mirror frames. That's the idea. Artists during this time liked to paint with pastel colors. A lot of the people painted in Rococo **portraits** were wearing very fancy pants and hats! The oil painting, *The Blue Boy,* by **Thomas Gainsborough** (British artist, 1727-1788) is a good example of Rococo style. Have you seen this painting?

35

How do artists slice and serve cheese to their friends?

With a palette knife

FUN FACT

A **palette knife** is actually not a knife! It looks like a tiny spatula for mixing and spreading paint. A **palette** is an artist's tool which traditionally looks like a flat piece of wood with a hole cut out so that the artist can put their oil paint colors on it and hold it while they paint. We usually see the flat wooden shape as a kind of oval. Some artists use the palette knife to actually paint directly on the canvas. It makes thick layers of paint right on the surface

36

**What is a pirate's favorite subject
in school?**

ARRRRRT!

FUN FACT

It's mine too! Maybe it's yours. Or maybe not. Enjoy getting to do art and appreciate it, but if it is not your favorite thing—no big. Find whatever is your favorite thing and do it your best! I teach some of my art students to play Chess. Some of them would rather play Chess than do art—and they are really great at Chess. Awesome.

37

**What happens when blue, green and
violet greet you at the door?**

You get a cool reception!

FUN FACT

A cool reception means they were not very excited to see you! However, in art, blue, green and violet (purple) are called the **cool colors** on the color wheel. (Not because they are snobs!) Why do you think they are called the cool colors? Do those colors remind you of anything?

38

What do you call Frankenstein's best artwork?

His monster-pieces!

FUN FACT

I love drawing monsters! You can make them any old way—shaggy or scribbly with snaggy teeth or fangs. Monsters can even look friendly and cute. I doodle them all the time. Try it. Draw some fun monsters.

39

What do you call a dog who loves to draw buildings?

A bark-itect

FUN FACT

Architecture is a huge part of the art world. In fact, my nephew is an architect in San Francisco. He loved drawing as a little boy and when he grew up he went to school to become a person who designs buildings. Maybe someday you will too. There are lots of ways to keep your love of art in what you do everyday.

40

What was Salvatore Dali's favorite breakfast?

Surreal and milk

FUN FACT

Salvador Dali (Spanish artist, 1904-1989) is one of my favorite artists! He had a funny sense of humor. I like that. His most famous painting may be *The Persistence of Memory* which shows a big clock that looks like it is melting. Supposedly he got this idea when one day he saw cheese melting on a plate and he combined it with the idea of symbolizing time being relative as in Einstein's theory. This style of art was called **Surrealism**. Have you seen his photo portrait of himself with a big fanciful mustache and googly eyes? It is as famous as any of his paintings!

41

Why wasn't black mad at gray?

He was feeling neutral.

FUN FACT

Some of you won't even think this is funny or clever. Maybe because you have never even heard about neutrals. Despite being extremely important in art, neutrals are not given much attention. True black, white and gray are scientifically (and in Art) not colors. They have no one specific color wavelength. People just refer to them as colors for convenience probably. I mean, they are in the crayon box, right? But now you know. They are **neutrals**!

42

Why did violet look confused?

Because she was pur-plexed!

102 ART JOKES FOR YOU

FUN FACT

You may have noticed already in this joke book that I have been pointing out that **violet** and **purple** are the same color. They are not two different colors, they are just two different names for the same color. When I talk about the rainbow colors I like to make sure to use the color name violet but it just means—purple!

43

**What did Claude Monet say when he
painted his final haystack?**

This is the last straw!

FUN FACT

Claude Monet (French artist, 1840-1926) was the founder of the style of art known as **Impressionism**. Everyone knows about his most famous water lily paintings—but did you know he painted humble haystacks a bunch of times? Why did he do that? He was fascinated with the appearance of **light** in his paintings. He painted haystacks at different times of the day to explore how the quality of different kinds of light affected the colors. Sometimes the haystacks were more pink, sometimes more blue or yellow.

44

What did Andy Warhol say to the candle that just burnt out?

That was your 15 minutes of flame!

FUN FACT

Andy Warhol (American artist, 1928-1987) was well known for being a part of the art style called **Pop Art** that was popular in the 1960's. He was also well known for his flamboyant personal style. A famous quote attributed to him was, "In the future, everyone will be world-famous for fifteen minutes." Do you think you will be famous for fifteen minutes?

45

What did Michelangelo say about his statue of David?

Never take this statue for granite!

FUN FACT

Michelangelo (Italian artist, 1475-1564) began sculpting the statue of David when he was only 26 years old. The huge piece of italian carrara marble (not granite!) had been sitting around abandoned and Michelangelo turned it into a masterpiece. Sometimes art students turn their noses up at certain supplies. I always say, you can make art with a stick in the mud. It's not about the materials—it's about the heart and skill of the artist!

46

**Why did someone honk at the
cube in the street?**

He looked like a road block

FUN FACT

A **cube** is a geometric form that looks like a block. It's very useful in drawing houses and furniture and things that have a block-like structure. **Rectangular prisms** look like stretched out cubes and are also helpful to draw things that look three dimensional.

47

What did the little pen say to the big piece of paper?

I ink I can! I ink I can!

FUN FACT

Artists can look at a big blank piece of paper and struggle to get an idea. It's okay.

Everyone has times like that. You are creative. You are more than enough. Breathe. *The Little Engine That Could* thought positive thoughts and didn't give up. So did the little pen. So can you!

48

Why did John James Audubon stop painting birds?

He didn't like their fowl language

FUN FACT

Foul language means not very kind words. **John James Audubon** (American artist, 1785-1851) was known for his highly detailed and beautiful illustrations of birds. He respected nature. He probably enjoyed all the sounds the birds made! He valued them.

49

Why did the pencil's friends stop hanging out with him?

They thought he was a little dull

FUN FACT

My pet peeve is—a dull pencil! All my art students want to sharpen their pencils. How about you?

50

Can you name a yummy bakery treat named after an Italian artist?

Donut-tello

FUN FACT

Kids know Renaissance artists by the **Teenage Mutant Ninja Turtles** names: Leonardo, Michelangelo, Raphael and Donatello! But do you know what kind of an artist Donatello was? **Donatello** (Italian artist, 1386-1466) was most known as a **sculptor**. One of his strengths was that he knew how to masterfully sculpt things out of many different materials such as stone, bronze, wood and more. His sculptures of people were beautifully proportioned. I don't think he ate donuts—but maybe some yummy Italian cannoli!

51

What did the primary paints chant to the other paints?

Can't make me!

FUN FACTS

Red, Yellow and Blue are the first or **primary colors** of
pigment paints. You cannot create or make these colors
by combining other colors. They are the starting colors
to mixing all the other colors. Try it. Mix up some colors
from the three primaries.

52

Why is a sphere such a different form to draw?

Because it's an oddball

FUN FACTS

A **sphere** is one of the basic geometric forms to learn to draw and shade when developing your drawing skills. In fact, if you draw a circle—it's just a flat looking circle shape until you shade it. Then it will appear more three dimensional and magically it becomes—a sphere! Try it. Draw a circle and then shade it so it looks like a sphere or ball.

**Why did the pencil draw
a horizontal line?**

It didn't want to line up!

FUN FACTS

A line standing up is called a **vertical** line. A line lying down on it's side is called a **horizontal** line. What is a line that is slanted called? That's right! A **diagonal** line! Try it. Draw a page full of different kinds of lines.

54

What did the little girl think of
Andy Warhol?

He was a soup-er artist!

FUN FACT

When most people think about **Andy Warhol**, the **Pop Art** artist, they think about his art image of a can of Cambell's soup! One time, an art student of mine said, "What's with the soup cans?!" after seeing that art print in my art class. Why do you think the artist Andy Warhol chose to make a piece of art with an image of a soup can? Do artists sometimes make art that has a special meaning? Do you?

55

Why did the pencil mark run by and quickly disappear?

It was going to a race

FUN FACT

My favorite kind of eraser is called a **kneaded eraser**. It looks like a glob of gray clay or chewed up gum, but it is soft and rubbery. It erases pencil marks without leaving all the little eraser crumbs that other erasers do. My art students get carried away sometimes molding their kneaded erasers into little sculptures. Try it. Get a kneaded eraser and make a little sculpture out of it! It's fun.

Who did Leonardo say he was calling on his cell phone?

i phone a Lisa

FUN FACT

The Mona Lisa by **Leonardo da Vinci** (Italian artist, 1452-1519) is the most famous painting in the world. It is housed in one of the greatest museums in the world called the **Louvre,** in France. Did you know the Mona Lisa was stolen right out of the Louvre in 1911? A handyman at the museum stole it and hid the painting in a trunk in his apartment in Italy. It was discovered there two years later and returned to the museum.

57

Want to hear a tissue paper joke?

Never mind—it's tearable!

FUN FACT

Tissue Paper is a light weight craft paper that comes in many colors and is often used in **collage** artwork because it is so easy to tear and make free form shapes.

5 8

Can you name an artist who sounds like he drinks a cup of Earl Grey in his fancy necktie?

Wayne Tea-bow

FUN FACT

Wayne Thiebaud (American artist, born 1920) is well known for his colorful paintings of cakes, pies and ice cream cones! Doesn't that sound delicious? Actually he paints many more things than that. But my art students always enjoy looking at his paintings of treats best. Try it. Think of a fun treat to draw and color.

59

**Can you name a cute little
Post-Impressionist critter?**

van Gopher

FUN FACT

Did you know that **Vincent van Gogh** (Dutch artist, 1853-1890) painted in a time that was just at the end of the other Impressionist painters, so he was called a **Post Impressionist**. Post is a word that means "after."

60

What Florentine painter painted a jar of jam on a seashell?

Botti-jelly

FUN FACT

Sandro Botticelli (Italian artist, 1445-1510) was a master painter from the time of the Early Renaissance. His best known work is the painting, *The Birth of Venus*. In this painting, the mythological goddess Venus is standing in a clamshell with her long hair blowing in the sea breeze.

61

Why did the paint blob wear a bandage?

It had a happy accident!

FUN FACT

Bob Ross (American artist, 1942-1995) was an art teacher on television from 1983 to 1994. His program was called *The Joy of Painting*. One of his famous quotes was: *We don't make mistakes, we have happy accidents.* I love this philosophy of making your artwork flow with whatever comes your way in the process. I always tell my students, see if you can work—whatever happened—into the flow of your piece somehow instead of starting over. You may be surprised how many times the artwork is completely awesome in the end.

62

Why was the pencil sticky with honey?

Because it was a two bee pencil

FUN FACT

My favorite all purpose drawing pencil is a soft number 2B. All my young students begin drawing classes with these. Without getting technical, I'm going to simplify what the letters B and H represent in the pencils. B means **SOFT**. H means **HARD**. A soft B pencil will be able to make a dark thicker line. A hard H pencil will be able to make a skinny light line. Numbers mean, "how much." The higher the number—the more it is. A 6B pencil is much softer than a 2B. A 4H pencil is much harder than a 2H. One of my favorite art teachers used to say, "Drawing with a 4H pencil is like using a nail!" That's pretty hard! What do you think an HB pencil is?

Why did the artist draw on the window?

Because he wanted to make his message very clear!

FUN FACT

Not every artist makes a message or a special meaning in every piece of their artwork. However, many artists do. The message isn't always clear. When you look at a piece of art, do you ever ask yourself, "Why did they do that?" Sometimes the artist has left information about the artwork for us to know why—sometimes not. That is one of the lovely mysterious things about art. We won't always know everything about a piece of art. Some of that is a secret just for the artist! Try it. Make a drawing with a message and only you know what it means.

64

**Why did the oil paints get mad
at the artist?**

He was trying to give them the brush off

FUN FACT

Oil paints are traditional art material. Many of the greatest paintings in the world were painted with oil paints, including some by Leonardo and Rembrandt. Oil paints are quite strong smelling. The only way to clean off this very permanent paint is with strong solvents. I have painted with oil paints, and what I liked best about them was that they were slow to dry so that you can make changes easily. I don't use them anymore because of the strong odor and solvents needed. I don't recommend them for children.

Why did the Gothic arch hate the Tudor one?

Because they were arch enemies!

FUN FACT

Did you know that you can tell a lot about old buildings by the kind of frames around doors and windows called **arches**? Some are pointed, some are rounded or other shapes. There is a long list of different types of arches popular at different times in history. Try it. Draw a little building with arches for doors and windows.

What happened when the red ship crashed into the black ship?

They were marooned

FUN FACT

"Marooned" means that they were stranded. But **maroon** also is the name of a color. It is a **shade** of dark red. Shades in art color theory are colors plus black. When you mix black with a color, it becomes a shade of that color. Color + Black = Shade. (Red + Black = Maroon)

67

Why do sculptors need mouthwash?

So they can gargoyle!

FUN FACT

Gargoyles are sculptures or carvings put on very old buildings that look like scary faces or creatures. They actually have a purpose. The gargoyles' mouths are drainspouts so that water and rain on the building will be spewed out away from the side of the building. That protects the building. Some people thought the gargoyles also protected the building by scaring away anything bad! Try it. Draw your own gargoyle.

68

What does a cylinder say to encourage you?

Yes, you can!

FUN FACT

A **cylinder** is a very useful form in drawing. It looks like a can. When I teach drawing I often say things like, "Draw it like a can of tuna." And my students know just what that looks like. A can of tuna is a short cylinder. A can of soda pop is a taller cylinder. I always teach a cylinder when we draw a mug of hot cocoa with marshmallows floating in it. Try it. Draw a mug of hot cocoa or a can of tuna.

Why didn't mint green get along with lime green?

Lime green was too intense!

FUN FACT

Do you know someone with an intense personality? I do. (Sometimes I am one myself!) That's okay. I get along with them anyway. They just want to be loved like you and me. But the difference between mint green and lime green is that mint green has white mixed in it. We call colors that have white mixed into them a **tint**. Color + White = Tint. We also say these colors have less **intensity** because their main color has been diluted with the white. Sometimes we call tints: **pastel colors**. Can you guess the name of the color that is the tint of red? That's right! It's pink.

70

Why did the lawyer like the painting in the courtroom?

Because it was non-objective

FUN FACT

Lawyers don't like people to object to their questions. However, in art, a painting that is **non-objective** means that there is no reference to anything real. It could just be a bunch of lines and shapes that don't represent anything. An **abstract** painting can be different than a non-objective one. Abstracts can begin with some kind of real thing and distort it or change its appearance. It doesn't have to be very recognizable though.

71

Why didn't red vote for green for President of the United States?

Because he wasn't in the primaries

FUN FACT

When you vote for someone in the United States for President they usually go through the primary election first. In color pigments, Red is a primary color and green is a secondary color.

72

Why did Rembrandt end up in poverty?

He was Baroque!

FUN FACT

Rembrandt van Rijn (Dutch artist, 1606-1669) did actually lose all of his money and went broke. Poverty means that you barely have enough money to buy food. The time in art history that he painted was called the **Baroque** period. Baroque was a style of fancy, expensive and elaborate designs for clothes and decorations. Rembrandt enjoyed fancy things and overspent. Lesson for us now? There is an art to finances. Save some of your money. Don't spend it all!

73

What would you name a colorful wolverine?

Hue Jackman

FUN FACT

Hue is another word for color. If you say the hue is blue, then you are saying the **color** is blue. Hugh Jackman is an actor famous for playing the role of the Marvel cartoon superhero, Wolverine, in movies. Try it. Draw a superhero. Color it any hues you want!

74

**What was the artist Bernini's
favorite pasta?**

Macaroni and Bees

FUN FACT

Bernini (Italian artist, 1598-1680) was one of the greatest artists of the Baroque period. He was most known for this incredible artistry as a **sculptor**. He was able to capture such beautiful details. Some of his most notable sculptures included bees as an element. This was because he was at one time the favored artist of the important Barberini family in Rome, Italy. It was their family crest that had three bees in it that he included sometimes. Bees are a symbol of beauty and hardwork. Try it. Draw a little bee.

75

Why did red give purple a tissue to wipe her tears?

Because he thought she was a little blue

FUN FACT

When people seem sad, sometimes we say they are feeling blue. **Purple**, also known as **Violet**, is a mixture of red and—blue!

76

**Why was the coloring book afraid of the
pencil drawing?**

He thought it looked a little sketchy!

FUN FACT

I love sketching free hand with pencil! I enjoy making scribbly lines. All kinds of lines actually. Smooth, rough, thick, thin, wavy, zig zag—all of them! **Sketching** helps me when I'm thinking about creating something. I love **sketchbooks**. I keep lots of them around to pick up and draw in when I feel like it. Coloring books are fun too. Some people think **coloring books** are silly. I don't. They just serve another purpose in art. Enjoy them both. Try it. Get a sketchbook and enjoy making your own doodles and sketches. Get a coloring book and enjoy filling in beautiful colors.

Why did Vincent buy a new car?

Because he let his van Gogh

FUN FACT

Another Vincent joke! I've studied a lot about the famous artist, Vincent van Gogh. I feel empathy for a lot of things that happened in Vincent's life. He tried really hard to be liked, and in spite of it, people had a hard time being his friend sometimes. Do you ever feel like this? It's okay. I think most of us feel discouraged sometimes. **You are unique.** You have something special to give the world. Vincent did. Sometimes I imagine him smiling at these jokes. Because somehow he knows we all love him and remember what a great guy he truly was.

78

Why did the square stop an argument?

Because he wanted all the sides
to be equal!

FUN FACT

Do you know the difference between a **square** and a **rectangle** shape? A **square** has four straight sides and each side is the exact same (equal) length! What about a rectangle?

79

What does an artist draw to get privacy in his studio?

The curtains

FUN FACT

I rarely draw curtains in my studio. I have blinds! Actually, if anything, I open the blinds because natural light is an artist's joy. In fact, **North light** is valued by artists the most. Windows that deliver light coming from the North are best because it is not extreme. It is a constant level of light so an artist doesn't have to worry about a lot of lighting changes as they paint. Some of the most famous paintings in the world were painted with North light.

80

Where does a cow go to see art?

A Mooooo-seum!

FUN FACT

Go to an **Art Museum**! I can't believe how many people never go to the museums that are so close to where they live. Start there. Will it be boring? Well. What are your expectations when you go? I guarantee you this—you will see things you have never seen before. Expect to see things new to you. Appreciate how humans all over the earth created amazing things to express themselves. Just seeing those things and being around them will grow you just a little. Try it! Go to a museum near to you. Then go to some far away, too.

81

Why were the art teacher's eyes crossed?

Because he couldn't control his pupils!

FUN FACT

A **pupil** is another word for a student. But it also means the black dot in the center of your eye. I never control my pupils! I actually do a fun experiment with my students when we draw eyes. I turn off the lights and then suddenly turn them back on. We all get excited to see how our pupils in our eyes shrink down! We talk about that. Then back to drawing pupils in the eyes. I find most of my students love doing art so much that they get into what I call the **art zone**. They are absorbed into their own art experience. No one is controlling them except themselves.

82

What did the street artist say when asked if he was a "pro" artist?

No. I'm a con artist.

FUN FACT

Will you be a professional artist someday? Someone who earns money for making art? Maybe. There are many amazing artists in the world. Some of them, like Vincent van Gogh, didn't make any money from doing their art. Interesting. Because now Vincent's paintings are worth millions of dollars. You might see some incredible **Street Art** by **i madonnari** artists for instance. These artists do beautiful chalk drawings on sidewalks and pavement. Their art is temporary. It gets washed away. Many of them do it for free. They love what they do. They are great artists—not con artists! That is just a joke. Try it. Get some chalk and make some i madonnari drawings on the sidewalk.

83

Did you get the joke about Michelangelo painting the Sistine Chapel?

No. It must have went over my head!

FUN FACT

How would you like to get up on a super tall scaffold, like a ladder, and look up for hours and paint the ceiling of a big church? Oh. By the way. Make it amazing. That is what the great **Michelangelo** (Italian artist, 1475-1564) did! His paintings in the Sistine Chapel in Italy are some of the most famous in the world. He did complain it gave him a pain in his neck though!

84

What did Micelangelo say after he finished painting the Sistine Chapel ceiling?

I got you covered!

FUN FACT

Michelangelo (Italian artist, 1475-1564) never wanted to paint this ceiling. He accepted the job but he really thought of himself as more of a **sculptor.** He didn't know much about painting a **fresco.** He literally learned on the job how to master this **fresco technique** of painting dry powdered pigments into damp plaster. He was a fast learner! But still, the ceiling took him about four years to paint.

85

Who was the friendliest Japanese artist?

Hokusai because he gave us a big wave!

FUN FACT

Katsushika Hokusai (Japanese artist, 1760-1849) gave us a big wave when he created the **print** he is most famous for, *The Great Wave of Kanagawa*. Most people don't realize that this famous work is not a painting. It was created by a printmaking technique called **woodblock printing**. You can make prints lots of ways. You can even scribble markers on the back of tin foil and then lay the tin foil with the marker side down onto a sheet of paper, press on it, and—ta-da! You made a print. Try it.

86

Hokusai waved hello, but how did the artist say good-bye?

Cyan-nara!

102 ART JOKES FOR YOU

FUN FACT

What a colorful way to say good-bye! **Cyan**, a blue-green hue, is a good color to think about when we think of Hokusai's *The Great Wave of Kanagawa.* Most people don't realize there is a focal point in the print, and it is not the wave. It is beautiful Mount Fuji right near the center of the composition. Did you know this wave print is only one of a series of prints called *Thirty-six Views of Mount Fuji* by the great Hokusai? Try it. Draw a big wave.

87

**What kind of art do skeletons
like to make?**

Skull-tures

FUN FACT

Georgia O'Keefe (American artist, 1887-1986) was not known for making sculpture. She is most known for making huge paintings of **flowers**. But she also painted paintings of bones and **skulls** of animals she found in the desert in New Mexico. They were interesting and beautiful. The bones were bleached out and looked like sculptures themselves. Try it. Find something sculptural from nature like a rock or a stick and draw it.

88

**How did Vincent van Gogh paint
Starry Night?**

Easel-y

FUN FACT

Vincent van Gogh (Dutch artist, 1853-1890) painted one of the world's favorite paintings, *The Starry Night*. It was not one of his personal favorite paintings. So funny that everyone else seems to love it now. He did often use an **easel** stand to do his paintings. His easel was made of wood and folded in so that he could move it around with him. Was painting *The Starry Night* easy for him? In letters to his beloved brother, Theo, he often talked about his paintings. Mostly he felt his paintings needed more work. Vincent was rarely satisfied with them. Do you ever feel like this? I do. Most artists struggle with the feeling that they will never be good enough. It's okay. It is just part of the process we sometimes go through that drives us forward. It may feel like we have a love-hate relationship with our art sometimes. But it is a passionate love—so much a part of us—so we keep going!

What did the yellow blob of paint say to the red blob?

You are one in Vermillion!

FUN FACT

Vermillion is the name of the color that is a brilliant red. Another name for this color might be **scarlet**. Not very many people use the word vermillion. I love it. I love all the different color names out there. **Chartreuse** is another color name I've always loved. Do you know what color that is? It's a bright yellow-green. I was sad when a few years ago they stopped making my favorite crayon color, **Dandelion.** Isn't that a great color name? A dark sunny yellow. Dandelion was super useful in art projects with my students when we used wax crayon techniques. Can you think of any other fun names for colors? Make some up!

What did one art print say to the other?

We're not in canvas anymore!

FUN FACT

I have a lot of art prints of famous paintings in my art room. Students know that they are not the original paintings. The originals were painted mostly on **canvas**. Raw canvas fabric is usually covered with a treatment coating called **gesso**. That helps it be stronger and hold the paint on the surface. You can go to a museum and see the original famous paintings on canvas. You can buy a printed reproduction of that original famous painting and have it for yourself! By the way, have you ever seen the Wizard of Oz?

91

What is a cat's favorite color?

Purrrr-ple!

102 ART JOKES FOR YOU

FUN FACT

You guessed this one didn't you?!

92

What architect could never be wrong?

Frank Lloyd Wright

FUN FACT

Frank Lloyd Wright (American artist,1867-1959) was most famous for designing buildings. He was a professional **architect**. He began a style of designing buildings known as the **Prairie** style. His style was about simplicity and an organic feel. I'm sure he made plenty of mistakes. All artists do. But he achieved a lot. Don't worry if you are not always right or if you make some mistakes. You learn something every time. Move on and do big things!

**What did he paintbrush say
to the artist Kandinsky?**

Stop going in circles!

Fun Fact

Wassily Kandinsky (Russian artist, 1866-1944) painted some of my favorite paintings with lots of circles! He also was a teacher at one of my favorite Art Schools in history, the **Bauhaus.** Much of Kandinsky's work was non-objective or abstract.

94

What do you call a forged painting of spaghetti?

An impasta!

FUN FACT

What is an art **forgery**? When someone passes a piece of artwork off saying it is an original piece created by a specific artist—and it's not! Why would they do that? To make money.

Forgery has been around for a long time and is still happening. Today, some people are copying other people's artwork off of the internet and selling it as their own without the original artist's permission. This is wrong. It is not a forgery, but it violates the original artist's **copyright.** It is always best to make your own original artwork!

Name a friendly colorful sea creature that represents all people?

Hue-manatee!

102 ART JOKES FOR YOU

FUN FACT

Manatees are **endangered animals**. They are very docile and friendly toward humans in general. I love animals. I love to draw them too. **Hue** is another word for color. It would be cool to draw a manatee—or any endangered animal—with fun colors. Humanity needs to help our animal friends thrive. Drawing them can help bring attention to them so we protect their right to share the earth with us. Try it. Draw an endangered animal.

96

What sign did Monet have by his water lily pond?

Frog parking only.
All others will be toad!

FUN FACT

Claude Monet (French artist, 1840-1926) had a beautiful water lily pond in his famous garden in Giverny, France. I'm sure some frogs enjoyed a floating moment from time to time on those lily pads! Frogs like to hang near water. Toads are a classification of frogs but prefer to venture out into the garden more. I enjoy drawing frogs and toads. There are some really colorful ones in the world. Try it. Draw a colorful frog or toad.

97

Why is avocado green a sad color?

Because it's pitiful

FUN FACT

Green comes in so many different variations! Avocado green is a wonderful, earthy green color. One of my favorites. There are so many Greens to use in your art: Forest Green, Lime Green Emerald Green, Mint Green and so many more. I always remind my art students about using lots of different green colors when they paint and color trees and plants that they see out the window. Does a tree have just one green color? Look. Where the light shines on it—it's a different green. Don't settle for just one green! Try it. Draw and color a tree—but use more than one green!

98

What did the paintbrush cheer before he painted?

Dip, Dip, Hooray!

FUN FACT

Painting is fun! The best way to paint is dip right in and don't be afraid to make a mistake or a mess. Will you make one? Maybe. Who cares! Get in there and have some fun.

Why was Green so angry looking across the color wheel?

He was always seeing red!

FUN FACT

Sometimes when people get angry they say that they were "seeing red." It's an old saying. Did you know that **colors** affect our body and feelings? It's true. There are scientific studies that prove it. If you sit in a room entirely painted red—your heart rate will go up. As an artist, it is important to understand colors. I teach a lot about color to my students. I adore colors. Who doesn't? Everyone deserves a healthy, happy dose of color every day! Try it. Put a color down on a paper. Stare at it. What do you feel? What does it remind you of?

100

Name a sea creature that likes Pop Art?

Andy Narwhal

FUN FACT

Do you like Narwhals? They are interesting sea creatures. I like their unicorn-like horn or tusk. In fact, it is a perfect creature to remind me of **Andy Warhol**, the **Pop artist**. He stood out in the world as someone who didn't follow or look like the crowd. A lot of people who like to do art like to dress more colorfully or different. Maybe they like to wear their hair different. Do you? Sometimes I do. But not always. That is just me. You don't have to look a certain way to be an artist. You can just be yourself.

101

What did the crayon say when the paint tube told him he had a crazy dream?

Don't worry. It's just a pigment of your imagination!

FUN FACT

Pigments are materials that make the appearance of color. In order to create paints of different colors, a formula of pigments have to be added to a base paint. A "figment of your imagination" means your mind just made it up, it's not real. Artists use the figments of their imaginations to create all kinds of art!

102

Why did the sharp drawing pencil have so many friends?

Because when they were with her, there was never a dull moment!

FUN FACT

You have come to the end of our *102 Art Jokes for You* journey! I hope you had fun and learned a lot about art. In fact, I hope that there was never a dull moment. Keep doing art, my friends! We are all in this artistic, colorful world together. **Try it. Keep being your awesome unique self and—-keep doing art!**

Made in the USA
Middletown, DE
12 October 2020

21798320R00117